W9-CTS-565

Pennycook Elementary School
3620 Fernwood Street
Vallejo, CA 94591
707-556-8590

HEALTHY AND HAPPY

Family and Friends

Louise Spilsbury

PowerKiDS
press

New York

Published in 2012 by The Rosen Publishing Group Inc.
29 East 21st Street, New York, NY 10010

Copyright © 2012 Wayland/
The Rosen Publishing Group, Inc.

All rights reserved. No part of this book may
be reproduced in any form without permission
from the publisher, except by a reviewer.

First Edition

Produced for Wayland by Calcium
Design: Paul Myerscough and Geoff Ward
Editor: Sarah Eason
Editor for Wayland: Joyce Bentley
Illustrations: Geoff Ward
Picture Research: Maria Joannou
Consultant: Sue Beck, MSc, BSc

Library of Congress Cataloging-in-Publication Data

Spilsbury, Louise.
Family and friends / by Louise Spilsbury. — 1st ed.
    p. cm. — (Healthy and happy)
Includes index.
ISBN 978-1-4488-5275-8 (library binding)
1. Families—Juvenile literature. 2. Friendship—Juvenile literature 3. Caring—Juvenile
literature. 4. Loss (Psychology)—Juvenile literature. I. Title.
HQ744.S69 2012
306.85—dc22

                            2010046263

Photographs: Fotolia: Jerome Berquez 6; Istockphoto: Digitalskillet 22, Mark Evans 16,
18, Rosemarie Gearhart 26, Sheryl Griffin 2, 10, Kim Gunkel 23, Bonnie Jacobs 13, Cat
London 21, Ekaterina Monakhova 25, Neustockimages 8, Muammer Mujdat Uzel 24;
Shutterstock: Elena Kouptsova-Vasic 17, Rob Marmion 7, Monkey Business Images 1, 4,
9, 15, 19, 20, Losevsky Pavel 12, Margot Petrowski 27, Lesley Rigg 11r, Jane September
11l, 14, Harald Høiland Tjøstheim 5.

Cover photograph: Shutterstock/Rob Marmion

Manufactured in China
CPSIA Compliance Information: Batch # WAS1102PK: For Further Information contact Rosen Publishing, New York, New York at 1-800-237-9932

Contents

Family and Friends 4

Families 6

Friendships 8

Caring for Each Other 10

Teamwork 12

Give and Take 14

Talking Together 16

Solving Problems 18

Being Kind 20

Respecting Differences 22

When You Lose Someone 24

Who Can Help? 26

Make a Friendship Bracelet 28

Family and Friends Topic Web 30

Glossary 31

Further Information and Web Sites 31

Index 32

Family and Friends

Family and friends are special. They care about us and we care about them. They are people that we can turn to for help and **advice**.

Different Relationships

Most people have many different **relationships**. You may have friends in your school or your street. There are different kinds of families, too. Some have two parents, others have one. Some children are **adopted** and others may live with a relative.

Friends are people we can share both happy and sad times with.

It's a
Fact!

A family tree is a picture that shows all the people in your family.

For most people around the world, family and friends are the most important things in their lives.

Same Feelings

People live in many different ways and in many different places. One thing that is the same for everyone is that family and friends are important to us. To be healthy and happy, we all need people who care about us!

Families

A family is made up of children and the adults who care for them. Families should take care of each other. How do they do this?

Family Support

The adults in families give children somewhere to live, food to eat, and clothes to wear. They also teach you how to behave. We share everyday times with our family, such as washing the dishes. We also share special times with them, like birthdays or going on vacation.

Families have fun, but they also work together.

Family Rules

Adults in a family make rules. These rules are there to keep you healthy and happy. As you get older, you may want to change some of the rules. Try to talk about this with your family in a friendly way. Remember, they only want the best for you.

HEALTHY HINTS

If you are unhappy at home or if you feel your family are unkind to you, try talking to a teacher or another adult you trust.

Different relatives make up your family, including aunts, uncles, and grandparents.

Friendships

Being a good friend and having good friends is an important part of keeping happy and healthy. Do you know what makes a good friend?

Good Friends

Good friends care about each other. They try to understand each other's feelings and moods. Good friends are happy for each other to have other friends. They trust each other to be **loyal**.

Some friends like the same things as you, but other friends may like different things.

You can be best friends with more than one person.

Friendship Problems

Friends can encourage you to try new things that are fun. Sometimes, a friend may try to **persuade** you to do something you do not want to do or that you know is wrong. This is not being a good friend. Friends can disagree without hurting each other's feelings, so say no to your friend and explain why.

HEALTHY HINTS

Try to make new friends wherever you go. Friends can make you happy and you will get something different from each new friendship.

Caring for Each Other

Family and friends show they care for each other in different ways. How do you show someone they are special to you?

Showing You Care

There are lots of different ways to show you care. You can show you care with the things you say. You could ask your dad how he feels if he has been sick. You could tell a friend what you like about them. Showing you care makes people feel happy.

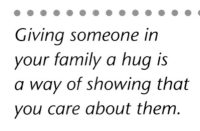

Giving someone in your family a hug is a way of showing that you care about them.

Showing Feelings

You can also show how you feel without words. Our faces let people see our feelings. People smile to show they are happy and frown to show they are cross or worried. The way we behave shows our feelings, too. A parent might show they care by giving you a kiss or a hug.

What feelings do you think these faces show?

It's a Fact!

You use more face **muscles** to frown than to smile, so it is easier to smile!

Teamwork

A team is a group of friends or family who work together to get something done. What makes a good team?

Working Together

People often work together when they have a job to do. Classmates work together to finish a project. A football team works together to score goals. To do the job well, teams share different roles. That way, everyone on the team does a fair share of the work.

Together, a team of people can do things that one person could not do alone.

It can feel great to be part of a team!

Making Teams Work

To make teams work, people share **decisions**. People on a team do what most of the team members want to do. You may be asked to do something you don't want to do, such as play a new position in a soccer game. But it may work out better for the team in the end.

HEALTHY HINTS

Many teams wear a uniform or T-shirts with their team name or logo. This helps members find each other in a crowd and it makes people feel that they are part of a team.

Give and Take

Part of being in a family and having friends is give and take. It means sharing and helping each other. How do you give and take?

Taking Turns

It is important to take turns in a game or wait for your turn to speak in class. Friends take turns to help each other, too. For instance, a friend might help you practice lines for a play. Then you take your turn and help them practice for a sports game or match.

When your parents make time to do fun things with you, such as swimming, think about what you could do for them in return.

Sharing Chores

There is a lot to do in a home, so families share **chores**. Children may take care of family pets, empty the wastebaskets, or do some cleaning. Although you may not like the idea of chores, most people find that helping others makes them feel good!

HEALTHY HINTS

You sometimes have to do chores that you don't like. Why not offer to do a job that you do like? That way you will get to do a chore you like and your family will be happy that you offered to help!

To make your family happy, you need to make time for your chores as well as for play.

Talking Together

Family and friends need time to talk. Talking together is a chance to share thoughts, secrets, and news. It also makes people feel close.

Speaking

When you are chatting with someone, try not to **interrupt** them. Wait for them to finish talking before you speak. Say what you think, but respect other people's ideas, too. It is also good to ask questions —especially if you don't understand something.

This girl is putting her hand up to ask her teacher a question.

The way people behave or move their hands when they talk helps you to understand what they are saying.

Listening

When you listen carefully, you find out more. A good listener hears what people say and concentrates on what the other person is saying, rather than thinking about what they will say next. When you listen well, you will also understand what the other person is feeling.

HEALTHY HINTS

Look at people when they are talking to you. It helps you to concentrate on what they are saying. It also shows them you are listening carefully.

Solving Problems

It is normal for friends and families to argue sometimes. After all, we all have our own **opinions**. It is important to know how to talk about them.

How to Argue

When you disagree with someone, it is okay to say so. Try to say you disagree in a friendly way, and be polite. Do not shout or say mean things. Talk calmly and quietly. Try to see the other person's point of view, even if you do not agree with them.

If someone is shouting at you, try not to shout back. Instead, walk away and tell them you would like to talk when they have calmed down.

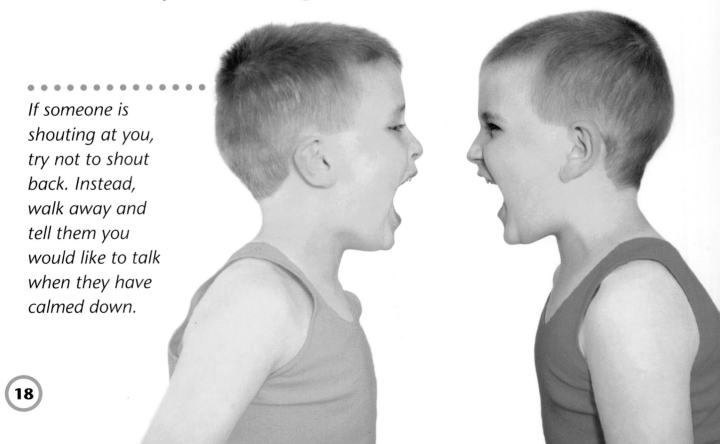

When you don't agree with someone, say so in a friendly way. That way, there will be no bad feelings afterward.

Fixing the Problem

If you quarrel with someone, the best thing to do is talk about it. Try to choose somewhere quiet to talk, away from other people. Before talking, think about what happened. Did you say or do something you could say sorry for? Saying sorry when you really mean it usually helps.

HEALTHY HINTS

When you feel really angry and want to shout, try going into another room. Take time out or count to 10 until you feel calm again.

Being Kind

The things we do and say affect our family and friends. When people are kind to each other, everyone feels happier.

How to Be Kind

Being kind means trying to understand how other people feel. Before you say something, think how you would feel if someone said it to you. It is good to tell people the things you like about them or the things they do well. There is no need to tell them the things you do not like about them!

Being mean to someone can make them feel sad, angry, and lonely.

Bullying

Bullying is when someone is very unkind to another person. A bully calls people names, hurts them, or makes them feel left out. If you see someone being bullied, try to help them. Helping others makes us feel good, too.

If you see someone sitting alone, the kind thing to do is to go and talk to them.

It's a Fact!

Tell your parent or teacher if you are being bullied. They will be able to help you to work things out.

21

Respecting Differences

The world is made up of many different kinds of people. All of us have the **right** to be happy and to be treated fairly.

Differences

People like different foods and different games. They have different-colored eyes and hair. Some people speak or dress differently, and some wear glasses or use a wheelchair. What people are like on the inside is more important than how they look.

It is fun to be friends with boys and girls and people who are older and younger than us, too.

Showing Respect

It is unfair to make fun of someone who is different from you, or to avoid playing with them. People feel unhappy when they are left out or treated unfairly. The world would be a boring place if we were all the same. Knowing different people is much more fun!

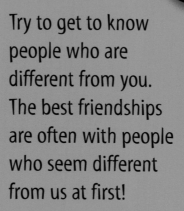

HEALTHY HINTS

Try to get to know people who are different from you. The best friendships are often with people who seem different from us at first!

We show people respect by being polite and kind to them.

23

When You Lose Someone

It is very hard to lose someone you care about. What happens when a friend moves to another school, a parent leaves home, or a pet dies?

Feelings

When someone leaves or dies, we miss them. It will help to talk about that person and your feelings with other people. Or you could write down how you feel in a letter, diary, or notebook.

When you first lose a friend or family member, you may feel sad, angry, and afraid.

Moving On

It is healthy to spend some time thinking about your loss, but it is unhealthy to do it all the time. You need to make time to do things that make you happy. Have a day out doing something fun. Find ways to make friends. You could join a club or take up a new sport.

HEALTHY HINTS

If you or a friend moves away, you can still keep in touch by phone, e-mail, or writing.

Finding new things to do is a good way to deal with loss.

Who Can Help?

People feel unhappy when they have problems with people they care about. Who can help if things are going wrong with family or friends?

Help for Friends

If you stop being friends with someone and cannot work things out, ask for help. Ask a parent, teacher, or older student to talk with you both. They can listen to what has happened and help you solve the problem.

Worrying about stuff is bad for you. Get help when you need it, so you can stay healthy and happy!

It's a Fact!

About 600 children call the Childhelp phone line every day. Most children call about problems in their family.

Talking to someone about a problem can make it better.

Family Troubles

Children need a family that cares for them and does not hurt them. If you are having problems at home, talk to a teacher or other adult you trust. Or you could call a helpline telephone number such as Childhelp. Some families go to a **family therapist**. This is someone who helps families to figure out their problems.

Make a Friendship Bracelet

You will need:
• embroidery thread, yarn, or cord in three different colors • scissors • tape

Why not show a friend you care by making them a friendship bracelet!

1. Cut two long pieces from each colored thread.

2. Hold all six threads at one end, with the pairs of colored thread together.

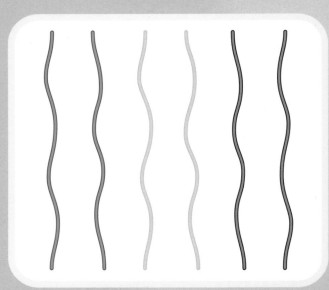

3. Tie a knot at one end of the six threads. Use tape to stick this knotted end to a table.

4. Separate the threads into the three pairs of colors and lay them flat.

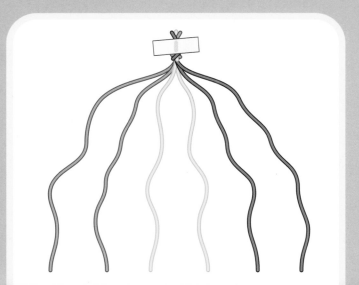

5. Braid the three pairs of threads together. To do this, take the pair of threads on the right and cross it over the middle pair of threads. Now do the same with the pair of threads on the left. Keep crossing the right and then the left pair of threads over, and pull the braid tight each time.

6. When you think the bracelet is long enough to go around your friend's wrist, tie a knot in the other end and remove the tape.

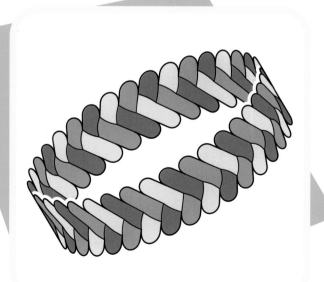

7. Now the bracelet is ready for your friend to wear!

Family and Friends Topic Web

Use this topic web to discover themes and ideas in subjects that are related to family and friends.

HEALTH EDUCATION
- Understanding that healthy relationships are good for us and keep us well.
- Understanding that unhealthy relationships are bad for us.
- How to be a good friend.
- How to show your feelings.
- How to listen to other people's feelings.
- Taking responsibility for the way in which you treat other people.
- Draw your own family tree.

GEOGRAPHY
- Understanding that family and friends are important to people everywhere.
- Understanding that friends can come from many different places and many different cultures.

FAMILY AND FRIENDS

ART AND DESIGN
- How to design and make a friendship bracelet from colored thread or fabric.

SCIENCE
- Understanding that some children have biological or birth parents and other children have adopted parents.

Glossary

adopted when a child is part of a family they were not born into

advice suggestion about what someone should do or say

chores jobs, such as housework or yard work

decisions choices made after thinking or talking about the best thing to do

family therapist someone who is trained to help families with problems

interrupt to stop someone else from speaking

loyal being faithful to someone and always supporting them

muscles parts of the body that make other body parts move

opinions feelings, thoughts, and ideas about something

persuade to make someone do something by telling them they should

relationships connections between people

right something that everyone should have by law or because it is fair

Further Information and Web Sites

Books

Being Healthy, Feeling Great: Relationships
by Robyn Hardyman
(PowerKids Press, 2010)

Healthy Body: Relationships
by Carol Ballard
(Blackbirch Books, 2004)

My Family: My Brothers and Sisters
by Emily Sebastian
(PowerKids Press, 2010)

Web Sites

Due to the changing nature of Internet links, PowerKids Press has developed an online list of Web sites related to the subject of this book. This site is updated regularly. Please use this link to access this list:
www.powerkidslinks.com/hah/family/

Index

adoption 4, 30, 31
advice 4, 26, 31
arguing 18

bullying 21, 27

caring 4, 5, 6, 7, 10–11
Childhelp 27, 31
chores 15, 31

family therapist 27, 31
family tree 5
feelings 9, 11, 17, 20, 24, 30
friendship bracelet 28–29, 30

helping 14, 20

kindness 20–21, 23

listening 17, 30
loss 24–25
loyalty 8, 31

problems 7, 9, 18–19, 26, 27

relationships 4, 31
relatives 7
respect 16, 22–23
rules 7

saying sorry 19
shouting 18, 19

taking turns 14
talking 16–17, 18, 19, 21
teamwork 12–13
"time out" 19